natural
revelations
THE ART OF SUSAN SWARTZ

Susan Swartz

natural revelations

THE ART OF SUSAN SWARTZ

WITH AN INTRODUCTION BY **ROBERT COLES**
AND CONCLUSION BY **JANE GOODALL**, PH.D. DBE

Jacket Art:
Purple Majesty 2, 2007, acrylic on linen, 72 x 72 inches

Title Page Art:
Vista [Autumn Twilight], 2001, acrylic on linen, 12 x 12 inches. Private collection.

Dedication Page Art:
Inner Silence, 2002, acrylic on linen, 48 x 36 inches. Private collection.

Contents Page Art:
In the Aspens, 1997, acrylic on linen, 52 x 74 inches. Private collection.

Page 108 Art:
The Waters Edge, 1999, acrylic on linen, 17 x 15 inches. Private collection.

Visit www.susanswartz.com

Designed by Traci O'Very Covey
Edited by Linda Bult

Printed by Carr Printing Company, Inc. Bountiful, Utah, United States in 2007
Bound by Schaffer Bindery

Library of Congress Cataloging-in-Publication Data

Swartz, Susan
Natural Revelations: The Art of Susan Swartz/Susan Swartz
with an introduction by Robert Coles and conclusion by Jane Goodall, Ph.d. DBE

ISBN 13: 978-0-615-15546-3

The book contains various quotes believed to be in the public domain, whose authors are cited internally.

dedication

To my parents, Peg and Lee Shallcross, for giving me life, love, and the courage to follow my passion.

To my husband, Jim, for sharing my life – for your inspiration, love, and total support of all my dreams.

To the joys of my life: Scott, Karin, and Kristin; their spouses Esmeralda, Nick, and Nick; and my grandchildren Jayme, Kayla, Kendra, Luca, Jake, Matti, Cassandra, Connor and Neta; who continue to bless me and make me the proudest and luckiest mom in the world.

To Millie Dienert, who has taught me there is no limit to the human spirit and to what faith can see us through.

To Laurie Westberg, for your tireless efforts, for your editorial assistance, and for sharing my dream so completely.

To Edna and Jim Pogue for your constant support and encouragement.

To Geralyn White Dreyfous for your constant encouragement and support – thank you for always being there.

And to the LORD for His daily inspiration, bounteous blessings, guidance, and unconditional love.

SUSAN SWARTZ
2007

contents

introduction

ROBERT COLES

the dreamy impressions of susan swartz

Susan Swartz's oil on canvas paintings render dream impressions taken from nature. In particular, her work is inspired by the Wasatch Mountain Range of Utah. Her compositions avoid postcard perspectives or stock imagery, and close-up visions of nature are offered in the form of color dances. Amid a deluge of disturbing reports regarding global warming, Swartz's paintings are decidedly affirmative testimonies to nature's beauty and its enduring qualities—its presence becomes for us mortals a precious and stirring and inviting companionship.

Her color schemes are Monet-influenced. Indeed, the viewer is hard-pressed to find pockets of focus or distraction within her designs. Continuous, fluid, and unified impressions run throughout her work. Swartz's unfettered impressions—in their sum, a kind of fervent, tenacious dream—spark optimism: a certain decided affirmation found in nature. The viewer is offered glimpses of aspen trees, of lilies, and of a first snowfall. Other paintings titled "First Light" or "Heaven" take the viewer into more reflective, even mystical realms. Swartz says, "I like to paint what God created." In a sense, she has let her painterly gifts be energized by her introspective inclinations, refined by philosophical study and contemplation.

GOLDEN PLAIN, 1997, ACRYLIC ON LINEN, 36 X 24 INCHES. PRIVATE COLLECTION.

A seamless cohesion is found in her Monet-influenced oil paintings. But unlike Monet, we are not given a perspective that enables one to make out or to discern haystacks, bridges, and man-made details. No locus is found that distracts or pulls at or summons our eyes. Rather, we encounter an overall portal that invites the entrance of our eyes: to behold tree groupings, pond surfaces, or more abstractly, a "first light"—all of which are shown in a manner at once modest and magical.

susan swartz, a natural eye

Susan Swartz's approach toward nature is reminiscent of the distance and angle of presentation that the color-master Eliot Porter chose to take with camera. Both Porter and Swartz use similar subject matter—pools in brooks, aspens, and rosebud trees. Neither image-maker focuses on sweeping vistas or long-distant panoramas. Both dwell on brilliant colors that play with the unpretentious and unassuming abstractions of nature that are close at hand, awaiting our eyes, minds, hearts: the ring of a meditative dance.

In his essay, "Nature," Emerson tells us that "the lover of nature" is one who "has retained the spirit of infancy even into the era of manhood." So the artist becomes psychoanalyst, Erik H. Erikson also told us: "Looking at the world around us, we sometimes find ourselves, learn from the outside what and (who) we are."

What follows are an American artist's responses to a part of her native land's terrain—shapes, colors, contents become for us what they were for her—a collective gift: the artist, whose eyes received so very much, enables us, who hold a book, to visit territory once beholden—now ours to enjoy, ponder.

In his essay, "What is Art?" Leo Tolstoy insists that "a work of art" ought "evoke that feeling…of spiritual union with another (the author) and with others (those who are also infected by it)." A great novelist was reminding himself, as well as his readers, that through words and pictures, we become a family of sorts: kin become (courtesy of a book, a painting, a photograph) a brotherhood, a sisterhood. An artist (in this instance, Susan Swartz) turns out to be a spiritual guide who awakens us to who we are and what we can learn from the world that we share with people, places, things.

Swartz says, "I like to paint what God created." In a sense, she has let her painterly gifts be energized by her introspective inclinations, refined by philosophical study and contemplation.

LIFELINES, 2006,
ACRYLIC ON LINEN, 36 X 60 INCHES.
PRIVATE COLLECTION.

about the artist

JIM SWARTZ

All of my adult life, I have been blessed to

SOLITUDE, 2004, ACRYLIC ON LINEN, 24 X 24 INCHES. PRIVATE COLLECTION.

be surrounded by Susan's creations and to be nurtured by her embracing joy of life. From the day that we met in 1965, Susan has never wavered in her love of nature or in her commitment to our family, to our environment, and to our God. Her positive view of all things in life sustains all of us who are fortunate enough to know her.

Now, with this book, Susan is sharing herself with an ever-widening audience, baring her soul for all to see—to be illuminated. This book, which documents Susan's recent work, is really a prayer and a love song to all future generations that they may inherit a world as beautiful as Susan now sees.

As we raised our three children—while I worked, and then while I was coming home on the train—Susan would paint long into the morning hours after the children were in bed. She was always totally happy in her world, recreating what she saw around us through her passionate and undistorted eyes.

Early on, she painted still lifes and children's and dogs' portraits. Then, landscapes from our travels in New England, California, France, and Africa; seascapes and sandpipers from our days on the shores of Long Beach Island; underwater scenes from the Red Sea, from Bermuda, and from the Great Barrier Reef. There were periods of birds, parrots, and eagles, and of bunnies and squirrels. And always flowers—baskets of flowers, flowers in lily patches, wildlife flowers from Albion Pass—flowers of all types. More recently, Susan has painted western landscapes and mountain trees. Very recently, she has moved to more and more abstraction.

But it has always been about nature—never cityscapes, never buildings, never man's creations—never portraits of people engaged in activities. Is man not perfect enough? Maybe. Susan paints nature and captures its unique perfection as only she can. She sees the world as a continuous series of God's perfect creations. Thankfully, she continues to create and to share these with us.

As Susan has nurtured our three children, Scott, Karin, and Kristin; and their mates, Esmeralda, Nick, and Nick; and now our nine grandchildren, she has become increasingly conscious of the need and, indeed, the mandate to preserve God's creations for them. Environmental protection, open spaces, sustainable growth, and spiritual development have all become of utmost importance to her psyche.

There is nothing more rewarding than seeing the morning sunlight on a tree-marked mountain or over a beach-lined expanse of open water or on fresh-falling snow on unspoiled land. Whatever we can do to preserve this vision for our children and grandchildren and others is more important than anything else we do.

We need to pay more attention to the sicknesses that come from not taking care of our environment. From chemicals to mercury poisoning to the onset of bird flu—we are increasingly being punished for not being conscious stewards of our environment. Susan demands this respect in her paintings: when we view them, we are constantly reminded of our charge. In her way, she chooses to look at the positive side and to not show the evil and the ugly. Rather, to show and to paint the natural beauty, and hopefully, each of us will come to see the good and be motivated to keep these places in our souls forever.

Susan chooses not to internalize and represent the dark and destructive side of the world in which we live. While not denying it, she would rather not fill her mind with watching violent movies or images of human tragedy or with dealing with the impossibilities of world conflict. A big supporter of the downtrodden and oppressed, she would rather focus her hopes and support on their spirit—to help them to a better life.

Susan has been given God's gift to present what was meant to be. We are extremely grateful for her brush, but more importantly, for her spirit. She has taken the time to always be in touch with nature and with her surroundings—we can all benefit from more of the same. When we travel, I am constantly amazed that I see buildings, road signs, and cars and that Susan sees trees, pastures, and flowers. How much I have missed in my life—how much all of us have missed.

Thank God for Susan, who allows us to momentarily return to nature and to enjoy it at a meaningful level. I hope that you enjoy these paintings as much as I have and that through them you come to know Susan's beautiful spirit and grace—that which I have been able to enjoy during my life.

May our grandchildren—Jayme, Kayla, Kendra, Luca, Jake, Cassandra, Matti, Connor, and Neta—be inspired by these paintings and continue with the charge to make the world a better place for us all.

TUMBLEWEEDS, 1999, ACRYLIC ON LINEN, 72 X 48 INCHES. PRIVATE COLLECTION.

spring

For lo, the winter is past,

the rain is over and gone;

The flowers appear on the earth,

the time of singing has come. . .

SONG OF SOLOMON, 2:11-1

TRANQUILITY, 2000, ACRYLIC ON LINEN, 20 X 20 INCHES. PRIVATE COLLECTION.

NATURE'S GRACE, 2002, ACRYLIC ON LINEN, 36 X 60 INCHES. PRIVATE COLLECTION.

The green leaves quiver
with the cooling wind,
and make a checkered
shadow on the ground;
under their sweet
shade let us sit. . .

WILLIAM SHAKESPEARE

STUDY IN GREEN, 2004, ACRYLIC ON LINEN CANVAS, 9 X 12 INCHES. PRIVATE COLLECTION.

The year's at the spring
And day's at the morn. . .
God's in His Heaven;
All's right with the world!

ROBERT BROWNING

ABOVE: **SPRING BURST,** 2000, ACRYLIC ON LINEN, 9 X 12 INCHES.
PRIVATE COLLECTION.
OPPOSITE: **AFTERNOON SHADOWS,** 2006, ACRYLIC ON LINEN, 30 X 30 INCHES.
PRIVATE COLLECTION.

CALIFORNIA VISTA, 1998, ACRYLIC ON LINEN, 60 X 36 INCHES.

Spring, summer, autumn, winter, . . .

Winds blow, suns set, and morning saith.

"Ye hills, put on your gold."

EBENEZER ELLIOTT "THE BUILDERS"

FOREST EDGE, 2005, ACRYLIC ON LINEN, 30 X 40 INCHES. PRIVATE COLLECTION.

SEASON'S HANDIWORK, 2003, ACRYLIC ON LINEN, 48 X 36 INCHES. PRIVATE COLLECTION. DEER VALLEY SYMPHONY SUMMER PROGRAM.

ASPENS & WILDFLOWERS, 1998, ACRYLIC ON LINEN, 36 X 60 INCHES. PRIVATE COLLECTION.

ALBION PASS, 1997, ACRYLIC ON LINEN, 17 X 13.5 INCHES. PRIVATE COLLECTION.

With a voice of promise
they come and part,
They sleep in dust
through the wintry hours,
They break forth in glory –
bring flowers,
bright flowers!

MRS. FELICIA D. HEMANS
"BRING FLOWERS"

DREAM FIELDS, 1997, ACRYLIC ON LINEN, 36 X 24 INCHES. PRIVATE COLLECTION.

Many eyes go through the meadow,
but few see the flowers in it.

RALPH WALDO EMERSON "THE NATURAL HISTORY OF INTELLECT"

GOLDEN STRAND, 1997, ACRYLIC ON LINEN, 24 X 18 INCHES. PRIVATE COLLECTION.

How does the meadow-flower its bloom unfold?

Because the lovely little flower is free down to its root, and, in that freedom bold;

WILLIAM WORDSWORTH "A POET!"

FLOWERING FIELDS [MEADOWS], 2000, ACRYLIC ON LINEN, 30 X 24 INCHES. PRIVATE COLLECTION.

SERENITY, 2000, ACRYLIC ON LINEN, 30 X 24 INCHES. PRIVATE COLLECTION.

So will I build my altar in the fields,

And the blue sky my fretted dome shall be,

And the sweet fragrance that the wild flower yields

Shall be the incense I will yield to thee.

SAMUEL TAYLOR COLERIDGE "TO NATURE"

ASPEN TWILIGHT [TWILIGHT], 2004, ACRYLIC ON LINEN, 30 X 40 INCHES. PRIVATE COLLECTION.

V ast and deep
the mountain
shadows grow.

SAMUEL ROGERS

PURPLE SHADOWS, 2004, ACRYLIC ON LINEN, 9 X 12 INCHES. PRIVATE COLLECTION.

PURPLE GRANDEUR, 2005, ACRYLIC ON LINEN, 24 X 36 INCHES.

summer

Lilies of each hue, – Golden and white, that float upon the waves, and court the wind.

WILLIAM WORDSWORTH "THE EXCURSION"

LILIES ON THE POND, 2006, ACRYLIC ON LINEN, 36 X 36 INCHES.

PURPLE MAJESTY, 2004, ACRYLIC ON LINEN, 12 X 9 INCHES. PRIVATE COLLECTION.

MORNING HARMONY, 2004, ACRYLIC ON LINEN, 12 X 9 INCHES. PRIVATE COLLECTION.

If I take the wings of the morning, and dwell in the uttermost parts of the sea; Even there shall thy hand lead me, and thy right hand shall hold me.

BIBLE, PSALMS, CH. CXXXIX, V. 9-10

ABOVE: **SOLITUDE IN RED #1**, 2006, ACRYLIC ON LINEN, 20 X 20 INCHES.

OPPOSITE: **SOLITUDE IN RED #2**, 2006, ACRYLIC ON LINEN, 20 X 20 INCHES. PRIVATE COLLECTION.

ABOVE: **IRIDESCENT REFLECTIONS,** 2004, ACRYLIC ON LINEN, 48 X 60 INCHES.
OPPOSITE: **SERENADE OF LILIES,** 2006, ACRYLIC ON LINEN, 72 X 72 INCHES.

WHITE TRANQUILITY, 2004, ACRYLIC ON LINEN, 36 X 24 INCHES. PRIVATE COLLECTION.

Let us open our leaves like a flower,
and be passive and receptive.

JOHN KEATS

WHITE IRIDESCENCE, 2004, ACRYLIC ON LINEN, 48 X 60 INCHES.
PRIVATE COLLECTION.

RAGELEJE, 1998, ACRYLIC ON LINEN, 12 X 9 INCHES. PRIVATE COLLECTION.

The sun from the western horizon

Like a magician extended his golden wand o'er the landscape;
. . . And sky and water . . . Seemed all on fire at the touch,
and melted and mingled together.

HENRY WADSWORTH LONGFELLOW, "EVANGELINE"

GENTLE MORNING, 2006, ACRYLIC ON LINEN, 36 X 36 INCHES.

The first hour of the morning is the rudder of the day.

HENRY WARD BEECHER

ABOVE: **CRIMSON REFLECTIONS**, 2007, ACRYLIC ON LINEN, 36 X 36 INCHES
OPPOSITE: **AFTER GLOW**, 2007, ACRYLIC ON LINEN, 36 X 36 INCHES

ABOVE: **WHITE LIGHT**, 2004, ACRYLIC ON LINEN, 24 X 36 INCHES.
OPPOSITE: **SUMMER MEDLEY**, 2005, ACRYLIC ON LINEN, 30 X 30 INCHES.

RED SAILS, 2007, ACRYLIC ON LINEN, 20 X 20 INCHES. PRIVATE COLLECTION.

DAY OF SAILING, 2004, ACRYLIC ON LINEN, 9 X 12 INCHES. PRIVATE COLLECTION.

ABOVE: **WATERS RADIANCE,** 2006, ACRYLIC ON LINEN, 45 X 45 INCHES. PRIVATE COLLECTION.
OPPOSITE: **SUMMER SERENADE,** 2006, ACRYLIC ON LINEN, 60 X 60 INCHES. PRIVATE COLLECTION.

Seas roll to waft me, suns to light me rise;

My footstool Earth, my canopy the skies.

ALEXANDER POPE "ESSAY ON MAN"

SUMMERS WARMTH, 1998, ACRYLIC ON LINEN, 36 X 36 INCHES. PRIVATE COLLECTION.

Summer. . . Filled was the air with a dreamy and magical light; and the landscape lay as if new created in all the freshness of childhood.

HENRY WADSWORTH LONGFELLOW

SUMMER DAY, 2005, ACRYLIC ON LINEN, 40 X 30 INCHES.

ABOVE: **FILTERED MIST**, 2006, ACRYLIC ON LINEN, 30 X 30 INCHES. PRIVATE COLLECTION.
OPPOSITE: **TURQUOISE SERENITY**, 2006, ACRYLIC ON LINEN, 30 X 30 INCHES.

The sky is the daily
bread of the eyes.

RALPH WALDO EMERSON

ABOVE: **SUNSET SAIL #1**, 2004, 20 X 20 INCHES, ACRYLIC ON LINEN. PRIVATE COLLECTION.
OPPOSITE: **SUNSET SAIL #2**, 2004, 20 X 20 INCHES, ACRYLIC ON LINEN, 20 X 20 INCHES. PRIVATE COLLECTION.

autumn

The dewy morn,
with breath all incense
and with cheek all bloom . . .
Glowing into day.

LORD BYRON "CHILDE HAROLD"

MISTY MORNING, 2005, ACRYLIC ON LINEN, 30 X 30 INCHES. PRIVATE COLLECTION.

The gilding of the Indian summer mellowed the pastures far and wide.

The russet woods stood ripe to be stripped, but yet were full of leaf.

CHARLOTTE BRONTE

ASPEN SERENITY, 2005, ACRYLIC ON LINEN, 40 X 30 INCHES.

There is a **harmony** in
autumn, and a
lustre in its **sky,**
Which through the
summer is not **heard**
or seen,
As if it **could** not be,
as if it had not **been.**

PERCY BYSSHE SHELLEY

ASPEN BRILLIANCE, 2000, ACRYLIC ON LINEN, 48 X 72 INCHES. PRIVATE COLLECTION.

ASPEN CLEARING, 2005, ACRYLIC ON LINEN, 20 X 20 INCHES. PRIVATE COLLECTION.

I went to the woods because I wished to live deliberately. . . and see if I could not learn what it had to teach, and not, when I came to die, discover that I had not lived.

HENRY DAVID THOREAU "WALDEN"

ASPEN SHIMMER, 2005, ACRYLIC ON LINEN, 20 X 20 INCHES. PRIVATE COLLECTION.

ABOVE: **COLORS AWRY,** 2006, ACRYLIC ON LINEN, 48 X 48 INCHES. PRIVATE COLLECTION.
OPPOSITE: **COLORED SPLENDOR,** 2006, ACRYLIC ON LINEN, 48 X 48 INCHES. PRIVATE COLLECTION.

A pillar'd shade High over-arch'd,

and echoing walks between.

JOHN MILTON "PARADISE LOST"

ASPENS IN FALL COLOR, 2003, ACRYLIC ON LINEN, 48 X 72 INCHES.
PRIVATE COLLECTION.

ASPEN STAND, 2004, ACRYLIC ON LINEN, 40 X 30 INCHES. PRIVATE COLLECTION.

It is not so much for its beauty that the forest makes
a claim upon men's hearts as for. . . That quality of air . . .
That so wonderfully changes and renews a weary spirit.

ROBERT LOUIS STEVENSON

SEPTEMBER PASSAGE, 2005, ACRYLIC ON LINEN, 18 X 18 INCHES. PRIVATE COLLECTION.

GOLDEN ETERNITY, 1999, ACRYLIC ON LINEN, 60 X 72 INCHES. PRIVATE COLLECTION.

FALL STUDY 2, 2005, ACRYLIC ON LINEN, 48 X 36 INCHES. PRIVATE COLLECTION.

In the woods, we return to reason and faith. There I feel that nothing can befall me in life. . . Which nature cannot repair.

RALPH WALDO EMERSON "NATURE"

HARVEST PASSION, 2005, ACRYLIC ON LINEN, 48 X 72 INCHES.
PRIVATE COLLECTION.

GOLDEN SILENCE, 2006, ACRYLIC ON LINEN, 36 X 48 INCHES. PRIVATE COLLECTION.

O_n woodlands ruddy

with autumn

The amber sunshine lies. . . .

WILLIAM CULLEN BRYANT "MY AUTUMN WALK"

ASPEN HOLLOW, 2006, ACRYLIC ON LINEN, 36 X 84 INCHES.
PRIVATE COLLECTION.

AMAZING GRACE, 2007, ACRYLIC ON LINEN, 72 X 72 INCHES.

PURPLE MAJESTY 2, 2007, ACRYLIC ON LINEN, 72 X 72 INCHES

FROM LEFT: **AUTUMN'S BOUNTY #1**, 2007, ACRYLIC ON LINEN, 48 X 72 INCHES, **AUTUMN'S BOUNTY #2**, 2007, ACRYLIC ON LINEN, 48 X 72 INCHES, **AUTUMN'S BOUNTY #3**, 2007, ACRYLIC ON LINEN, 48 X 72 INCHES.

The trees, though not fully clothed, were in that delightful state, when further beauty is known to be at hand, and when. . . more yet remains for the imagination.

JANE AUSTEN

FALL RADIANCE, 2000, ACRYLIC ON LINEN, 36 X 48 INCHES. PRIVATE COLLECTION.

FALL SERENADE, 2006, ACRYLIC ON LINEN, 60 X 36 INCHES. PRIVATE COLLECTION.

N o Spring nor Summer

Beauty hath such grace as I have seen in one Autumnal face.

JOHN DONNE "ELEGY IX: THE AUTUMNAL"

Delicious autumn!
My very soul is wedded to it,
and if I were a bird
I would fly about
the earth seeking
the successive autumns.

GEORGE ELLIOT

ABOVE: **RED OCTOBER,** 2004, ACRYLIC ON LINEN, 36 X 84 INCHES. PRIVATE COLLECTION.
OPPOSITE: **MORNING CALM,** 2004, ACRYLIC ON LINEN, 48 X 48 INCHES. PRIVATE COLLECTION.
HARVARD DIVINITY SCHOOL EXHIBITION POSTER.

And they were canopied
by the blue sky,
So cloudless, clear, and
purely beautiful,
That God alone
was to be seen in Heaven.

LORD BYRON "THE DREAM"

BLUE SKY, 2005, ACRYLIC ON LINEN, 24 X 36 INCHES. PRIVATE COLLECTION.

GOLDEN ASPENS II, 2003, ACRYLIC ON LINEN, 48 X 60 INCHES. PRIVATE COLLECTION.

winter

Nature is full of genious . . .

so that not a **snowflake** escapes

its **fashioning** hand.

HENRY DAVID THOREAU

EVERGREENS AMID THE ASPENS, 2002, ACRYLIC ON LINEN, 48 X 48 INCHES. PRIVATE COLLECTION.

What unnumbered cathedrals has He reared in the forest shades, vast and grand. . . haunted evermore be tremulous music. . .

HENRY WARD BEECHER

ABOVE: **ASPEN SYMPHONY,** 2005, ACRYLIC ON LINEN, 24 X 36 INCHES. PRIVATE COLLECTION.
OPPOSITE: **FIRST FLAKES,** 2003, ACRYLIC ON LINEN, 30 X 30 INCHES. PRIVATE COLLECTION.

ABOVE: **APPROACHING STORM**, 2001, ACRYLIC ON LINEN, 30 X 30 INCHES. PRIVATE COLLECTION.
OPPOSITE: **PINE SPLENDOR**, 1998, ACRYLIC ON LINEN, 30 X 48 INCHES. PRIVATE COLLECTION.

Now all the tree-tops
lay asleep,
Like green waves
on the sea,
As Still as the
silent deep
The ocean-woods may be.

PERCY BYSSHE SHELLEY
"THE RECOLLECTION II"

IN THE GLOAMING, 2001, ACRYLIC ON LINEN, 48 X 72 INCHES. PRIVATE COLLECTION.

TOGETHER WE STAND, 2001, ACRYLIC ON LINEN, 20 X 20 INCHES. PRIVATE COLLECTION.

ABOVE: **THE FIRE WITHIN**, 2001, ACRYLIC ON LINEN, 24 X 36 INCHES. PRIVATE COLLECTION.
COVER FOR CULTURAL OLYMPICS.
OPPOSITE: **SOLDIER HOLLOW**, 2001, ACRYLIC ON LINEN, 60 X 60 INCHES. PRIVATE COLLECTION.
COMMISSIONED BY THE SALT LAKE 2002 WINTER OLYMPICS.

ABOVE: **WINTER SUN**, 1999, ACRYLIC ON LINEN, 60 X 72 INCHES. PRIVATE COLLECTION.
OPPOSITE: **CASCADE SPRINGS**, 2001, ACRYLIC ON LINEN, 36 X 60 INCHES. PRIVATE COLLECTION.
COMMISSIONED BY THE SALT LAKE 2002 WINTER OLYMPICS.

ABOVE: **STAND ALONE**, 2001, ACRYLIC ON LINEN, 24 X 36 INCHES. PRIVATE COLLECTION.
OPPOSITE: **CRISP WINTERS MORNING**, 2002, ACRYLIC ON LINEN, 40 X 40 INCHES.
PRIVATE COLLECTION.

The trees were gazing up into the sky,

Their bare arms stretched in prayer for the snows.

ALEXANDER SMITH "A LIFE-DRAMA SCENE II"

EVENING CALM, 2006, ACRYLIC ON LINEN, 40 X 30 INCHES. PRIVATE COLLECTION.

How gently rock yon poplars high against the reach of primrose sky
With heaven's pale candles stored.

JEAN INGELOW "SUPPER AT THE MILL" (A SONG)

OCTOBER CHILL, 2002, ACRYLIC ON LINEN, 20 X 20 INCHES. PRIVATE COLLECTION.

conclusion

DR. JANE GOODALL, PH.D. DBE

WATERLILIES #5, 2003, ACRYLIC ON LINEN, 20 X 20 INCHES. PRIVATE COLLECTION.

We live in dark times.

I have three grandchildren, and when I think how we have damaged this planet since I was their age, I feel quite desperate. What has gone wrong? Traditionally, many indigenous people made major decisions based on "How will this affect our people seven generations into the future?"—today, decisions are too often based on "How will this affect the next shareholders meeting?"

The dangerous consequences of this short-sightedness, coupled with mushrooming human population growth, has led to pollution of air, land, and water; the growing of food with poisonous chemicals; the destruction of nature; the extinction of species; and the reckless consumption of precious natural resources such as trees, oil, and water.

Fortunately, there is growing awareness of the danger, and many groups and individuals are taking action to make the world a better place. The Jane Goodall Institute's Roots & Shoots program for youth, now present in nearly 100 countries, encourages young people to work for positive change through "knowledge,

CHANGING SEASON, 2003, ACRYLIC ON LINEN, 30 X 30 INCHES. PRIVATE COLLECTION.

THE REFUGE, 1999, ACRYLIC ON LINEN, 40 X 30 INCHES. PRIVATE COLLECTION.

compassion, and action." Each group, after learning about the social and environmental problems around them, chooses projects that will benefit people, animals, and the environment. And these groups are networking around the world so that they come to understand that individual involvement and local action is truly tackling problems globally.

Susan Swartz shares my concern for the future of life on this planet. Each of her paintings richly illustrates the beauty of our world—from snow-covered slopes to rustic vineyards and country gardens. This exquisite art will appeal to everyone who loves nature and will bring the beauty into the homes of those who live in the city.

And Susan encourages us not only to experience and savor these images of nature, but also to do what we can to save nature itself. How tragic it would be if people living in the future were to look at these paintings and know that the settings that inspired them were no more. How they might yearn to experience, for themselves, the richness of sound and scent and color. We, who live today, must not allow such a future to come to pass. No, we must roll up our sleeves, and each do our part to save the beauty of nature for those who follow. And we must act now— before it is too late.

DR. JANE GOODALL, DBE
FOUNDER - THE JANE GOODALL INSTITUTE
UN MESSENGER OF PEACE

www.janegoodall.org